Apocryphal Musings

Melissa Treglia

APOCRYPHAL MUSINGS

Digital release:
1st Edition / Smashwords © August 2015
2nd Edition / Amazon © July 2018

Print release:
1st Edition / CreateSpace © November 2016
2nd Edition / Amazon © August 2018

ISBN 978-1542419178
ASIN 1542419174

For my mother,
whose gift of music came to me
in the rhythm of language.

INTRODUCTION

apocryphal *(uh-POK-ruh-full)* adj.
1. Of questionable authorship, authenticity or sanction.
2. Of, pertaining to or similar to the Apocrypha, a set of 14 books not considered canonical to Christian belief. They are included in the Septuagint and the Vulgate Bibles, but left out of the Protestant Bible.
3. Believed to be false, spurious or counterfeit.
Origin: c. 1400 Middle English, based on the Greek *apókryphos* ("hidden", "unknown")

musings *(MYOO-zings)* noun.
1. Thoughts, comments or reflections upon a subject.
2. Dreams, fantasies or idle fancies.
Origin: c. 1400 Middle English *musen* ("to mutter", "to gaze at", "to be astonished"), based on the Greek *Mousai* (term for the Nine Muses, goddesses who preside over art and science)

A writer's poetry reflects the thoughts hidden in one's mind: fantasies that delight us, feelings that overwhelm us, or terrors that stalk us in the night—thoughts that may not be true, but are real to us just the same. Poetry is a universal language that all can relate to; like music, it reflects our inner selves out to the full view of others, so that those who share our feelings will recognize they are not alone.

I always knew I wanted to be a published writer. In what way and in what genre, I still cannot say. I have written numerous stories and poems since around the time I was old enough to pick up a pencil and write my own name.

But having total strangers read my work is another matter. I have no difficulty whatsoever sharing my endeavors in fiction (be they of the original or fan-work variety), but my poetry is another matter. My poetry is my own and remains very personal to me, and there are some works which I have kept solely to myself, reluctant to share my soul in full view of the world.

Until now.

I have only recently made peace with my own reticence; the hope of my work resonating with others is worth the risk that comes of unzipping my flesh to reveal the heart and mind dwelling within. This collection you are reading now covers more than two-thirds of my lifetime—from my "salad days" (when I was young and green) to the current year (now being much older and, hopefully, a little wiser). The pieces are in a somewhat random order, and bookended by two hymns to the Muses I have written specifically for this collection.

As a writer struggling in her craft to be recognized, I can't help but thank Amazon, CreateSpace and Smashwords for permitting aspiring writers like me to publish our work directly to the masses, sans middleman or the cost of a vanity publisher. And thank YOU (yes, you, the person reading this humble collection of poetry right now) for being interested in my work enough to purchase this compilation.

I hope you delight in the discovery of each piece (from the silly to the sublime, and from the romantic to the cynical) as I did when I first wrote them, and come to treasure this book which was two decades in the making.

Melissa Treglia

Invocation of the Nine Muses

Calliope
Name now fairground music
Once loveliest of voice
Singing battles won and heroes immortal
Strength of legend in your song

Clio
With a second sight of long ago
Times past brought on your wings
You whisper in the ears of your acolytes
Who sweep pages for bits of history

Erato
Sing of the passion flowing
Through red veins and beating hearts
Bleeding out emotions tender
Into song of timeless love

Euterpe
Wild in her own dance with flute
Gyrating to the beat of unseen drums
Only poets know your music
Of beat, meter and rhyme

Melpomene
Sad lady with care-drawn face
Pluck beauty from lines of tragedy
Help to face inner demons

And our own mortality

Polyhymnia
Your name means "many songs"
You sing out the geometry of chance
The mathematics of life and its breadth
Order within the chaos of creativity

Terpsichore
Dance with me, oh light-footed lady
Shout your joy and shimmy your hips
As the drum beats shake stale air
Into a river of breath

Thalia
Full of smiles and jokes
Always festive no matter the season
Bringing joy wherever you go
Giving us laughter after tears dry

Urania
Look to the sky with me
As stars shine down on us, wondering
How very small were are in this world
As comets and spaceflot lead the dance

Nine sisters
Full of life and laughter
Of song and music, tears and longing
Sit with me awhile under your Father's sky

And sing with me, daughters of Memory

Written May 2015/Previously unreleased

Private Hell

All that I have left through these many years
Are bruises, heartache and traces of tears
The innocence is gone—nothing's the same
Shattered pieces are all that remain

Dare to look upon the damage you've done
Do you feel more like a man now that you've won?
I've waved the white flag, admitted my defeat
What might have been never will be

Take away the sadness within me
Give me release
Set me free from this private hell
Give me peace
All that I am is nothing without you
Come back to me
Set me free

Written September 2011/Previously unreleased

Addicted

Don't need no mary jane
Don't need no cocaine
To make me feel the pain you do
It's more than I can explain
And I know I must be insane
To still feel love for you

Logically
I know you're no good for me
But you have such an effect on me
I'm drowning and I just can't see
I can barely breathe
'Cos you've taken over me

Written September 2011/Previously unreleased

Lullaby

Deep in the forest, by the spring
A little calf curls up to sleep
The shadows fall as the nightbird sings
And the owl his watch will keep

So sleep tight, my dearest boy
Let not the darkness hold sway
For I am here, my pride and joy
To guard you till the light of day

Rest well, till night breathes its last
For we are the same flesh and blood
My every heartbeat holds you fast
With the strength and power of my love

So sleep tight, my little child
Let not worries crease your brow
May all your dreams be soft and mild
And you wake to the robin on her bough

All your dreams will be soft and mild
And you'll wake to the robin on her bough

Written September 2012/Previously unreleased

Roses in December

I can still remember
That cold, still January day
You were such a charmer
And I didn't know what to say
Amidst the winter chill
I could feel your warm embrace
When spring drove the dark away
The only light I needed was in your face

Amidst today's cold and gloom
Your smile I can still remember
The Gods bestow upon us love
So we may have roses in December

For awhile the world was bright
With the sweet colors of possibility
Love made my spirit whole and light
I felt beautiful with the love given me
But somehow in time you changed
Or perhaps I was the one who did
The darkness returned with sharp words
And among angry clouds, the summer sun hid

It wasn't all dark and gloom
I'm trying hard to remember
That Fate gives us love
So we have roses in December

It's been years since then
And my skies are still cold and gray
Still, the roses are safely in my heart
Against the somber Christmas day

Amidst the cold and gloom
Your kiss I can still remember
I now know I experienced love
So I'd still have roses this December

Written December 2009

Six Years

It has been six years...
Since his long shadow darkened her doorway.
Since he waited in the pouring rain to see her.

It has been six years...
Since she knew the agony of old fear.
Since she knew the joy of young love.

It has been six years...
Since he made her feel so hideous.
Since he made her feel so beautiful.

It has been six years...
And she prays she'll never hurt again.
And she hopes she'll know love again.

It has been six years...
Since she has seen his face in the shadows.
Since she has heard his voice in her ears.

It has been six years...
Since she heard him screaming in the house.
Since she heard him play music in the car.

It has been six years...
Since he hit her with his words and fists.
Since she hit him with a pillow and giggles.

It has been six years...
Since his embrace was her prison.
Since his embrace was her refuge.

It has been six years...
Since she has recoiled at his touch.
Since she has melted with his kiss.

It has been six years...
Since his fingers probed in lecherous want.
Since his fingers explored in playful tickles.

It has been six years...
Since oral sex was an act of servitude.
Since oral sex was an act of homage.

It has been six years...
Since her heart was held captive.
Since her heart was set free.

It has been six years...
And his torture still lingers.
And his laughter still remains.

It has been six years...
And the pain has not vanished.
And the love has only deepened.

It has been six years...
And he is still her only hate.
And he is still her only love.

It has been six years...
Since he was her jailer.
Since he was her savior.

It has been six years...
And she prays he'll never return.
And she hopes one day he will.

Written October 2009

We Have to Love

We loved each other because of the brightest of summers
Which painted the world, the city, love itself in pink

We loved each other because of life and our big dreams
Big dreams we built together around our little Paradise

We loved each other because of an instant, a moment
Because of the time, place and ambiance of our little world

We have to love each other despite the time lost
Despite the junk of our past clinging to us like old rags

We have to love each other despite the dreams lost
The dreams which faded when Adam and Eve left their
Paradise

We have to love each other despite the rain
The rain that drowns our sunny days with grey skies

We have to love each other despite the neediness
The wont of indulgent hearts and years of comfortable
habit

We have to love each other in spite of the worst
Despite our endless strategies and countless problems

We have to love each other in spite of the decades
In spite of our declining bodies and waning memories

We have to love each other in spite of many things
But we can no longer ignore the need to see them
differently

We have to love each other because love transforms itself
Love itself and everything around us has changed

We have to love each other in spite of all things
Because it's when we love selflessly that we are whole

Written June 2009

Demon in Me

Feeding the empty pit in my stomach
While my heart starves
Taking comfort in texture and taste
For lack of comforting words or arms
This demon in me is insatiable
Needs to be driven out
So much harm I do to myself
Hating myself
Driven by this need
To fill the void
Then purge it of what has been taken
The cycle never ends
Purgatory for my soul unworthy of love
Ana and Mia whisper seductive lies
Their bony, wasted arms around my shoulders
Their lies are too easy to believe
Can I be strong enough
To climb out of this darkness I've sunk into?

Written May 2008

Angel

With soft paws you padded
In this shabby apartment
Your white fur a light in my life
But now you are gone
Gone in body
But never in spirit

You have traded in your white paws
For a pair of beautiful wings
My dear dove-tailed companion
Loving and kind spirit
You will truly be missed

May those in the great beyond
Know the joy and love I knew
Through your humble spirit
And as you fly among the stars
And dance upon the clouds
Remember that I loved you

Written February 2008

This Much is True

Lying in bed, the morning sun on my face
But in my heart exists a dark, empty space
The day is beginning but my world is crumbling
And I find myself stumbling, fumbling
I long for your voice, your glance, your touch
For whispered words that meant so much

I can't help but think of how much I need you
If I could just have one more chance to see you
If I'd have known we'd never be together
I would've stayed in your arms forever
I'm so lonely without you, running from the pain
I can't shake it without you to take it from me again

I'd give anything to drown in your eyes again
But all I can do is think back and remember when
Without you here, images form in my mind
Wistful dreams of once upon a time
One smile from you would light up my night
Give colour to the clouds, and brighten the sunlight

Without you, the shadows surround me
Without you, gloom is all around me
You're tucked away in my heart and haunt my dreams
Without you, my soul silently screams
Each day goes by more dismal than the last
And it feels like eternity for every hour that's passed

From my memory, your face will never fade
And I'll never forget the love we made
I foolishly believed that I had the upper hand
Now I wish I could make you understand
I can't make it without you, I'm just not that strong
But I'm just strong enough to admit that I was so wrong

For a start, I'd give you the whole world
I'd give anything at all to just be your girl
Baby have a heart, I'm on my knees begging you
Let me show you how much I need you
I don't just miss your touch, I miss everything about you
This much is true; I'm still madly in love with you

Written August 2007

Why?

Why can't I let go?
Why do I still feel for him after so long?
Why does his name still enter my mind?
Why does anything he does matter to me anymore?
Why am I still hanging on to this bare thread of hope?

What is the point to any of this?
When will I breathe on my own again?
When can I hope for myself again?
When can I stop believing his promise to come back?
Why can't I see that promise for the lie it is?

Why am I still sad, when I stopped crying long ago?
Why am I merely existing without him instead of living?
Why can't I believe love will find me again?
When will my heart mend?
When will he be just a distant memory, a half-forgotten
face?

Why am I still waiting?

Written July 2007

Love Waits

It would be my fondest wish
To turn back the hands of time
So I may gaze into your eyes again
To erase the shading of days gone by
From eyes, lips, skin and hair
To sit in the sun watching the waves
Crash against the seashore
As we did so long ago together
To know your thoughts as I knew then
And knowing that you were mine
To live eternity within a moment
Love still waits here...

Written February 2007

Depression

Lost within myself
I seek solace from the pain
Unable to lift my head
To cast away the dark clouds surrounding me
I prayed for an unseen God to lift the curse
And His silence has killed my faith
I cast many a spell to exorcise the demons
Yet I remain shackled by them
Primal fear prevents me from seeking better
And that there is no better than this
Unable to love or be loved
I am in love only with my sadness
I am a slave to my own needs
Imprisoned by my many losses
There is a faint light in the distance
A dying flicker of hope
I fear the numbness of intoxicants
And of apathy caused by modern medicine
All I feel is pain
But at least I can feel something
But all the more painful
Is that I once knew happiness

Written December 2006

Forsaken

Eloi, Eloi, lama sabachthani?

Why
Why have you forsaken me?
You were never there
When I needed you to save me

Why
Why are you so far away?
Why are you not here
With only silence when I pray?

You have forsaken me
Cast down among demons
You left me to my pain
You have abandoned me
When I needed you
Rejected, broken again

Why
Can't you hear my scream?
Were you not sent down
For my agonies to redeem?

Why
Can't you help heal my wounds?
Or am I not good enough
For you to bother to be around?

You have forsaken me
Cast into a pit of despair
You left me to my pain
You have abandoned me
Where were you when I was
Rejected, broken again?

Eloi, Eloi, lama sabachthani?

Father, into your hands
I commend my spirit
Save me, save me!
Father, hear my cries
Why have you
Forsaken me, forsaken me?

You have forsaken me
Cast into your hell
You left me to my pain
You have abandoned me
Leaving me to die
Rejected, broken again

You never loved me
You never loved me
You never loved me
You aren't real
You aren't real
You were never real

It is finished...

Written June 2006

The Engagement (For Britney and Tom)

Standing in the distance
I watch as you both start a new life together
Expectant, thrilled and nervous
As you prepare for a lauded beginning

As time passes in your marriage
May the ties that bind never be broken
May your souls find comfort in one another
May your fears be always eased in companionship
And your inner longings be satisfied

May you never get so caught up in the mundane
That you neglect the miraculous
And when things turn to anger and tears
May you never remain upset long

May your home be filled with love
The sound of laughter and the smell of good food
May your families remain at peace
And never tread on your bond

When the summer of your love
Turns to winter's grey
May you remain as strong in your love
As you were from the first

In times of trouble
May your bond strengthen

And as the world changes around you
May your love be untouched by time

May you never run out
Of things to talk about
Of food in your cupboards
Of clothes on your backs

May the stars always shine brighter
When you are in each other's arms
And may the sun feel warmer
When you gaze at the clouds as one

May you always be surrounded
By those who love you
And those who support you
In times of both need and plenty

May you never long for much
And be rich in heart
And as you glance behind you
Know we are standing there

Blessings upon you, Britney and Tom
As your new life together begins
May your love always be
The stuff dreams are made of

Written November 2005

The Wait

Minutes falling like feathers from a great height
I ponder the mystery of their passage
And of the relativity theory

Why does time pass so slowly
When one is still?
Why does it pass by quickly
When one is in motion?

Earlier there were phone calls and laughter
Gossip and playful chatter
But now all is still and quiet
Save for machine hum and soft rock radio

I sit and I think
The night will be long
Just as the night before it
How I wish to go home

But I've only just left
And will be here for such few hours
But these hours will crawl snail-like
I wish to talk to my friend again
So time can pass quickly here
But duty calls

Restless yet still
I wait for the end of the day

Written November 2005

The Tryst

My love comes to me in the night
Face obscured by darkness
Shying away from the light
That remains in my house

My love takes me in his arms
After beckoning me forth
His soft voice charms me
And I fall under his spell

My love kisses me deeply
Holding me fast to him
I can feel he needs me
To quench the fire in him

The lights dim to nothing
As he lays me on the bed
And when it's me he's covering
No lights are needed then

In the darkness, I feel his lips
Pressed against my neck
With a nibble, with a kiss
As his hand slips into me

I gasp at his touch
Cool against my burning skin
Sensations course through me much

And it has been so long

I whisper his name
As I feel the sharpness of his fangs
Plunge into my vein
As his fingers plunge within me

Pleasure/pain floods me, I gasp
Then he pulls away
His voice an earthy rasp
Asking if I want more

I plead for him love me
As mortals may do
I cling to him above me
His name on my lips

He silences me with another kiss
As he slowly undresses me
Soon we are sinking into sweet bliss
Until dawn comes

With the curtains down
He sleeps in my arms
If this love is wrong
I don't want to be right

Written November 2005

The Paramour

I am many things, I have been many people
But none please me more than this life
For the one I love is with me here
And her heart beats only for me

She is the sunlight of my darkness
The rays of light peeking through storm clouds
Her smile is the only light I need
Her love is my only religion

With her, I am no monster or fiend
But a mere man
She breathes life into my cold body
And passion into my lifeless heart

Oh! how I long to feel her touch
The warmth against my skin
To hear her whisper my name
Or her fervent cries of pleasure

But this darkness within me could hurt her
Though I love her so dearly
It is the monster within me
That could be her undoing

I wish nothing more than
To be everything she wants and desires
To give her the love she needs

But I could hurt her in my eagerness

I can never satisfy my love for her
So I keep my distance
And I can only content myself
With my dormant dreams

In sleep, she is mine and mine alone
And I am able to give her all the passion within me
Without fear
Until our dalliances tire us

My angel of light
How can you love this demon?
I have fallen from grace
And am redeemed only by your ethereal love

If I should hurt you, my love
Please forgive me
For there is no love quite like yours
And you deserve better than I

Written November 2005

The Hunter

Darkness is with me, inside of me
Part of me
Like an old friend, it's always there
Seething in quiet rage

Yet beauty lies in the heart of darkness
A deadly game
In hot pursuit of warm blood and flesh
Stalking the night

The beauty in darkness
Is in the fatal dance
Driven by lust and hunger
The taking of sweet life

Yet this dance does not last
Longer than nightfall
For when the darkness turns to daylight
The chase ends

From darkness into daylight
I meet my end

Written November 2005

The Real Me

You've come to me based on an ideal
Believing your own fantasy real
But I am flawed, merely human
I am the common creature known as woman
I never lied about my being, my choice
And I've spoken with no other than my own voice
I wear little makeup as I've no obsession
With that unattainable thing called perfection

I do not care to chase men as sport
And with womanizers I have no rapport
You say that I am without a clue
But that's not the case—so here's a tip for you
If I interest you, then accept me for who I am
For your unrealistic vision I don't give a damn

I am stubborn, my laughter is rich
I am intelligent and a sarcastic bitch
I have no patience for pettiness or fools
And I refuse to play by your rules

I am more gentle and kind than angry, you see
And love is a many-splendoured thing for me
When I give my heart, it's for eternity
I lock inside the one I love and throw away the key
But it's not through words that I demonstrate passion
I do so only through my actions

I feel more deeply than you'll ever know
And I care much more than I can show
On children and animals I bestow affection
And I give the disaffected special attention
I oft befriend the misunderstood
Perhaps I care more than anyone could
I defy the barriers of race, color or creed
Breaking through to those most in need

To my friends, I am counselor and confidante
With me they share their feelings and wants
They know placing a secret in my possession
Is like entering a church's booth of confession

I am normally not one to play up my abilities
As I tend to live my life quietly
But in your search for perfection, it pains me to see
That you have mistaken, misjudged the real me
But I also realize one thing that could also be true
Perhaps I am too much woman for you

Written November 2005

The Ex

Give me your reasons
Give me your lies
Give me your deceit
For my spirit's demise
Give me your jaded view
Eliminate me from your chosen few

Deny me your attentions
Deny me your love
Break me down
So I'll not rise above
Use me as the forgotten toy
Of an ADHD'd little boy

Abuse me
Curse my very name
Make me your punching bag
It's all just the same
You've become no different, child
From the very thing you revile

Your insecurity betrays you
Your demons slay you
Your darkness calls to you
Your fears fall upon you
You have plummeted from grace
In time, your memory will be erased

I am not angry
I feel no fear
No sense of betrayal lingers
Nor the sting of tears
Time has been my healer
Experience is my teacher

I am strong
I am beautiful
I am not broken
I am not pitiful
I am not left wanting
Nor am I needy
I am not longing
With my affections, I'm not greedy

Love will come to me once again
I know I won't need you in the end

Written November 2005

Ambition

Lightning has struck
They say it only does so once
My fortune has taken a turn
My reality has changed
Bending with my will
But the fire in me still burns

A sip from this jade cup
A small taste of success
Flirting with the endless possibilities
That now stand before me
Yet that taste is not enough to quench
My parched desires

But I will wait
Bide my time
Exercise patience
Go through the daily grind
Keeping to myself
Working as I should
Playing by the rules
Keeping to standards of what is good

My time will come eventually
I know this is true
For now I am content
And every day is a learning experience
I still hold fast to my dreams

There are so many
And I can never truly let go

I will not be content being nameless forever
That is not my destiny
My whole life is before me
It is only a matter of time
Before I break free from the herd
Into the freedom of self-realization
Until conception claims reality

I am not normal
Was never meant to be
What I am meant for
Is only to be myself

My time will come
I wait for it with bated breath
As the clock ticks off the end of each day
I am patient
My entire life leads up to this distant hope
Someday I will claim it as my own

Written November 2005

Alone Once Again

I'm looking for a trace, a mark
Some sort of sign somewhere
To make all my dreams come true
So I can love once again
Young and naive I was
When sex was a way to pass the time
And I thought I didn't need anyone
Those days are far behind

I'm alone once again
The friends I knew are gone
Alone once again
Nobody to talk to on the phone
Alone once again
I have no place to call home
Alone once again
Without a love to call my own

It feels so strange
And I'm not quite sure
Of the feelings deep inside me
I feel so insecure
The cure for this ailment
Is love that calls to me from afar
But it's so unclear to see
And I don't know where you are

I'm alone once again

I'm tired of being by myself
Alone once again
While my heart stays on a shelf
Alone once again
I don't want this anymore
Alone once again
Where's the one I adore?

Oh, how I wish I could fly
Into a pair of arms that will comfort me
I played the game, ended up the fool
Needing someone to hold me
I don't wanna live by myself anymore
But what can I do?
I never stopped loving you

What happened to the dreams we shared?
What happened to the days you cared?
I'd give anything to bring them back again
Just to stop the pain I feel within

I'm alone once again
Loneliness is my only friend
Alone once again
And I may be till the end
Alone once again
Here I am without love
Alone once again
Can I ever rise above?

Alone once again

My heart can't take anymore of this
Alone once again
Clinging to a faded moment of bliss
Alone once again
With the emptiness inside
Alone once again
With the tears I try to hide

Alone once again
With only a vain thread of hope alive
Alone once again
I can't keep living this lie
Alone once again
Without a soul to comfort me
Alone once again
With only a vague memory

Written August 2005

An Ocean Away

It took so long to realize
What it was all for
Never understood
Why you waited at the door
I never imagined
That it would come to this
That we'd be worlds apart
After a brief moment of bliss

And now
After all this time
I wish
That you still were mine
And I wait
An ocean away
I just wish
I was with you today

I know I stumbled
Everyone makes mistakes
And for my ingratitude
This was the price I paid
I want to make it up to you
Someway, somehow
After everything we've been through
All I can do now

Is wait

After all this time
And wish
That you still were mine
As I wait
An ocean away
I wish
I was with you today

I know it's not easy to forget
The broken promises and the pain
But if I just had one wish to claim
I turn back the hands of time
So you could be mine
But all I can do now is wait

And so I wait
Like you have before
And I wish
I could have you once more
But I can only wait
An ocean away
Yet I wish
We were still together today

Written August 2005

You'll Miss Me (When I'm Gone)

The winds of change course through time
Seasons come, then pass by
There's a time to reap and a time to sow
A time to hold on and a time to let go
And as a chapter of my life draws to a close
Time carries us onward, and I know
You'll miss me when I'm gone

Months passed by since I first met you
What odds could've brought together us two
That I'd learn to love you with each passing day
Only to be forced to break away
And though you deny it, I know the truth
Deep down you feel the same as I do
And you'll miss me when I'm gone

You'll miss the late-night talks
The sound of my voice
You'll miss teasing me
And my every odd choice
The way I laugh at your jokes
How I tag along
When you go out for a smoke
You'll miss my attention
The look in my eyes
My affection
The moment we have to say goodbye

How I adore the sound of your voice
Your smile
Your devil-may-care bravado
Your youth, carefree and wild
And I've had so many sleepless nights
Just once, I wish I could hold you tight
And never have to let go
I wish I could hear you say "I love you too"

And though you'll never say it
I know you'll miss me when I'm gone
Deep down you know it's true
You're gonna miss me when I'm gone

And you know I'll miss you
I'm gonna miss you when I'm gone

Written April 2005

Distant Memories

The words I write are here
Within this hole in my heart
Words I wish I could give you
Were our two souls not apart
Sleep cannot seem to find me
Within this space of time
As the light brings a new day
My thoughts linger behind

Everything was so perfect
Or so it seemed to me
Now nothing is as it should be

And so I fall apart
Unable to stop the ache in my heart
And you no longer seem to care
Or realize that I'm still there
I cannot reconcile this
As every day there's something I miss
About what we had shared completely
What once was is just a memory

I just can't help but wonder
How you could ever say goodbye
You never gave an answer
When I asked you why
And thoughts of you still linger
Though I've tried to move on

And I can't help but mourn
Because what we had is gone

It all could've been so perfect
At least it seemed to me
Now nothing is the way it should be

And I just fall apart
I can't stop this ache in my heart
And you just don't seem to care
Or recognize that I'm still there
I can't get over this
Every day I understand what I miss
About what existed between you and me
What was is now just a memory

I just can't seem to forget
The things you said or the day we met
I can't help but wonder if
Your actions I could at least forgive

I had it all envisioned so perfectly
Of what was supposed to be
Now nothing's as it should be
Anymore

'Cos I just fall apart
Unable to stop this pain in my heart
Knowing you no longer seem to care
Or remember that I was always there
I just can't let go of this

As every day there's more that I miss
About what might have been for you and me
But what was is now only a distant memory

Written January 2005

Fall is...

A kaleidoscope of oranges, reds, yellows, and browns on
falling leaves.
A slight chill in the wind warning that winter is not too far
away.
A time for kids to return to school, lunchboxes and
textbooks in hand.
A transition. A time of change.
The end of summer.
A time to harvest goods that the farmers have grown.
A time to jump and do cartwheels into piles of leaves.
A time to enjoy the brevity of youth.
An end, a beginning.

Written September 2002

To Mom with Love (Little Girl, Big Dreams)

I'm a young girl with ambitious dreams
Nothing looks as it seems
Although I seem rather plain outside
I'm a future Diva on the inside
I want to sing for people, great and small
I want to write songs for them all
People may say I'm crazy, naive or blind
But I could never leave my dreams behind
I'm tired of people saying what's best for me
I just want them to see
I'm not gonna give up, my dreams'll come true
And if you've supported my future, I won't forget you
In ten years or so, I'll buy you a mansion and a phat car
But the greatest gift I can give you is to be your shining star
Mom, I'll never forget the way you took care of me
And one day I'm sure you'll see
That the music you sang was what began my life
And that music gets me through the darkest nights
So thank you Mom, for believing in me
And one day, it'll be you and me
Singing together on stage with musicians and vocalists
I know that wherever there's music, happiness is
And you and me together, will be as it is in my dreams
All I must do is find the ways and means....

Written May 2001

Love's Symphony

Love's symphony
An orchestral of boundless passion
The heart's strings playing a tune of endless longing
Trumpets sounding whenever your lover is near
An eternal dance of desire
To a timeless melody and seductive rhythm
Never-ending but always changing
Altering
Adjusting to the passage of time

The fire burns
With a thirst that water cannot quench or drown
An interminable ache within the body and the soul
Longing to hear your lover's voice
Seductive in its gentleness
Feel his touch
Cool against your burning skin
You are set aflame
By the passion that binds you to him

Hunger
Of the flesh, of the spirit, of the blood
A craving to become one with your lover
Animal instinct merging with a human soul
A desire to unite
To feel what he feels
To know what he knows
To see what he sees

To become him as he becomes you

Written October 2002

A Daughter's Song (For My Mom)

From the time I took my first faltering steps
Your watchful eyes always guided me
You remember the first time I smiled
My first word is ingrained in your memory
You pushed me to succeed at whatever I set my mind to
Such a stubborn little girl I was - didn't want to hear
But you only tried to do what was best for me
It's because you love me that I'm still here

When things went wrong
I expected you to fix it all
Didn't realize how human you are
It was faith that conquered it all
Now I know how special you are to me
Now that I've grown I can see
All that you did for me

So much has changed for you and me
Time may have turned your hair to grey
But you're still the same person inside
And I'll be your little girl till my dying day
You watched me grow from a child to a woman
I didn't tell you then but I'm not ashamed to say so now
That your support means so much to me
And it's because you love me I know how

To love and to care
'Cos you showed me what love is

There is nothing like a mother's love
And as your daughter I feel so blessed
You showed me all I needed to know
Because you helped me to grow
Now I understand, I know

You taught me how to laugh and dried my tears
You were there to pick me up when I fell
You always stood by me through those years
And we've both gone through so much hell
But I just wanted you to know
How much I love you

Written January 2003

It Could Have Been You

When I wake up early every morn
To see the man whose children I've borne
The face I see is not the one I adore
And yet he has to me given his *amour*
But I realize, as I always do
That he could have been you

The face I see at the breakfast table
I try to glance at, yet I'm unable
Though I've grown used to it, it's true
It still could have been you

When I go to work, the place is desolate
Ever since you decided to relocate
No cures to test or bullets to remove
And no troubled vampire heart to soothe

Each day follows the same as the one before
My life has become such a bore!
And so I wonder in my daily solitude
Where are you?

And when I come home every evening
A part of me is still scheming
Of how I might find you wherever you are
And flee from this life, into your arms
But I know one thing is true
I'll never be able to find you

So I sink into my bed
Thoughts of you still in my head
And cursing every new wrinkle and grey hair
It just isn't fair!

And I wonder why you're not here
Why I can't have you near
You promised me forever
And said we'll always be together
And I wonder if you ever really cared
Was it really love that we had shared?

Sleep begins to claim me, I find
And so I try to still my mind
And try not to think of you
Of how my heart's been broken in two

As I finally turn off the light
And kiss my husband goodnight
This one thing remains true
He could have...
Should have been you

Written December 2004

I'll Survive

Hiding myself from everyone
Feeling so out of place
All I want is to be loved by someone
But to see my real "face"
You must be patient with me
As I strip away the layers
Of falsehoods meant for others to see
I have to know will you still love me

On a shore that only I know
Waves slap the jetty
Seagulls cry
The stars sing an eerie anthem
That I don't want to hear

As a child, I was always ill
Loneliness was my constant companion
And Death never seemed far behind
I've always felt like nobody cares
But I've survived
Though I'm still sensitive inside
No one will forget my name
Or what I have to say

I won't go down without a fight
I won't let them win
I've fought for my life since it begun
And I won't let anyone take it from me

I'll survive
I'll survive
I'll be the last one standing

Written August 2000

I Am...

I am a quiet girl who dreams of fame
I wonder if my songs will make it onto Billboard's Hot 100
I hear thousands of loyal fans screaming my name
I see myself in the Stade de France in Paris
I want to be a great singer and songwriter
I am a quiet girl who dreams of fame

I pretend I'm recording a track in a well-kept studio
I feel the sharp intake of breath as I sing another line
I touch the sheet music on the stand
I worry about making a mistake
I cry because I can't tell anyone about my dreams yet
I am a quiet girl who dreams of fame

I understand that a lot of hard work is required
I say I only want to be appreciated for what I can do
I dream of sharing my music, my story, with the world
I try to overcome my shyness and fears of inadequacy
I hope that everyone will have their own dreams come true
I am a quiet girl who dreams of fame

Written September 2000

Isn't it Just

Isn't it just a shame
How people can take advantage of life
Isn't it just so sad
How we can overlook the needy ones
Isn't it just so angering
How people can walk all over you
Isn't it just so maddening
How people can be so cruel

But just walk away
Fight the tears and be strong
'Cos when all is said and done
You'll be the last one standing

Written March 2000

So Many Times

So many times I've tried
To let my feelings show
But you walked away from me
And left me feeling low
Why can't I get myself
To be strong without you
'Cos I can't go on anymore
With a man that's untrue

So many times I've said
I'd live only for me
But you made me feel weak
With a feeling that won't let me be
Why can't I get myself
To live my life without you
'Cos I can't go on no more
With a man who makes me blue

So many times I let myself be weak
Now can I be strong enough
To say the words I need to speak?

Written March 2000

The Lovers

A kiss
A caress to his face
A gentle grasp of her hand
A tender embrace
Hands in each other's hair
Undressing each other like butterflies from a cocoon
Fingers against bare skin
Whispered words and promises
A stolen moment

Written May 2001

Empty Within

A faint breath of rage, a deep sorrow in her heart
As, all alone, she cries in the dark
For the prince to whom she had sworn her love and life
For whom she longs to become lover and wife
Sees in his view the face of another woman
Seemingly oblivious to the one who loves him
She weeps openly at a certain sad song
And every night leaves her still awake at dawn
Sleep holds no comfort for her any longer
As his face and voice continue to haunt her
Sleep is her torment, a demise of the damned
The price of her sins delivered by fate's cruel hand
Yet only in her dreams is he solely hers
And only meant for her his touch, his words
Yet the dream will fade when she opens her eyes
And the truth of her existence is realized
The moment she looks in the mirror to see
Empty within, shards of me...

Written July 2003

Forgotten

I am invisible, no more than air.
You look at me without seeing me.
Just staring right through me,
As if I were a mere ghost,
A phantasmic shade from the past.
The wounds I carry are never visible,
But hidden well.
You deride the tears I cry,
Yet in the same breath call me "friend".
You fail to see I am still here,
A body made of bone, sinew, flesh and blood.
I am lifeless and joyless to you,
An echo in a barren wasteland.

Yet have I not shared your every joy and sorrow
As if it were my own?
Has it not been my comfort you have sought?
My shoulder you have cried on?
My ears in which you have confided?
Have I not given you moments to speak
Of life and death, height and depths
And have your meaning understood?
Does my silent devotion mean nothing to you?
Was I ever real to you?

Or am I just the remnants of a fading dream...

Written June 2004

Damaged

There is a break in my reality,
The cause of which I cannot see.
Memories of the past fade into my mind,
Causing my perception to drift back in time.

What was it I did to see all of this?
What curse did infiltrate into my former bliss?
Was I the cause of all the wrongdoing as you claim?
Or do you condemn me to shift the blame?

Was I your plaything that you could use and discard?
Or am I to believe for you saying sorry is too hard?
Am I the root of your grave despair?
Or am I a nameless face for which you do not care?

Am I to believe you meant no insult
When accepting your lies makes my conscience revolt?
For there is no greater curse than knowing you're being
used,
Manipulated, mocked, beaten and abused.

Written November 2004

Purgatory

Bathed in the blood of crimes unforgiven
I give naught but what was once mine
A history of lies and death follow me
Sealed within the hands of time
Condemned to a fate worse than death
The light to me now forever lost
As I am driven to steal the blood of life
In the sea of self-loathing I am tossed

Forgotten to all and even to myself
I dwell within my self-made hell
Will I find the salvation for which I've striven?
The simple truth is only time may tell

Written November 2004

Balancing Act

Poetry is an outlet given to me only
So I may foretell my intentions
From the depths of my soul come to light
This form of self-expression

Woven into delicate verse
Is the source of my passion and drive
For I cannot say such in my reality
And the music of rhyme keeps me alive

Within the confines of pen and paper
I question all that may be
I hope, I wonder, I dream, I pray
Of what lies ahead for me

Such thoughts are not to be voiced
For such is my forcéd pact
And so in my life I conceal my thoughts
Performing my balancing act

Written November 2004

Hallowe'en

A time of pumpkin picking
Trick-or-treating
Jack-o-lantern carving
Leaf pile jumping
Costume wearing
Scary movie watching
Holiday fun

The town abounds with
Creepy creatures
(Not quite so) vicious vampires
Wicked witches
Scary spirits
Wild werewolves
Who just want candy!

Written October 2002

Ice

Ice
The opposite of fire
A natural element
Cold to the touch
Chilling the fingers
As cubes dropped into a cup
But also a powerful destructive force
In the form of an iceberg
Always so cold
Bobbing on the surface
Then slowly melting
In the heat of the day

Written September 2002

I'm Not Perfect, And That's Okay

I'm not perfect and that's okay
'Cos God didn't make me that way
People will judge me but that's all right
It won't disturb my sleep at night
Some people may not like my voice
They don't have to listen, they have a choice
Some people may not like my clothes
But I like my style and that's the way it goes
Some people may not like what I have to say
It's my opinion, but I'm sorry they feel that way
Some might have a problem with the way I am
But the truth is I don't give a damn
Some people may think that insults will hurt me
Their words are based on ignorance, they don't know me
My personality may rub some the wrong way
But that's all right, I won't see them another day
Words may sting, judgment may be cruel
But they can't change my point of view
For my beliefs people may try to knock me down
But I'm a survivor and I'll stick around
People may taunt, tease, jest and mock me
But they'll get theirs eventually
I may not be as attractive as a movie star
But it's perseverance that'll get me far
I'm only human so it's okay
If there's a few dark clouds on my sunny day
Just as long as I can say honestly

"I'm glad and proud to be just me"

Written March 2002

Untitled (Silly Supermodel)

Silly supermodel
Sucking up umpteen weight loss pills
Instead of eating a balanced breakfast
You'd rather starve than eat a steak
Silly prostitute
Fucking dirty old men who watch ancient porn
Who finally come to you for your services
Because they can't get it any other way
Silly teen popstar
Screwing record label managers to get a deal
Letting them give it to you any way they want
When the real artists can't catch a break
Silly Hollywood actress
Demanding the stars on a diamond chain
Wanting a shitload of cash for your bit part
And getting it all only because you're popular
You all suck!

Written February 2002

Quand Je Vois Ton Sourire

Quand je vois ton sourire
Le ciel et soleil me sourit
Les étoiles me chante
Dans le milieu de la nuit

Quand tu m'embrasse
Je sais tu m'aimes
Je suis libre
Quand tu comprend

Quand je regarde tes yeux
Je suis libre
Tu peux lire mon esprit
Comme un livre

Written December 2001

Untitled (Never Thought)

I wish I could go back to the way things used to be
But what I know now I just didn't see
I never thought you'd beat me black and blue
Never thought I'd cry because of you
I never imagined I could be so vulnerable
I always thought you were so lovable
Now I know you're really just another jerk
Funny though, I've tried to make it work

Never thought love would hurt
Never thought you'd make me cry
Never thought I'd live like this
Never thought it'd be a nightmare

Who am I to say what is right or what is wrong
But I've been a puppet on your strings for far too long
What I need now is some time to rest
Because all you got was the best
But you gave me nothing in return
And when you're dead, I hope you burn
My life has been hell since I first met you
Now it's time to say good-bye and forget you

Never had the strength to walk away
Never had the courage to fight back
Never is a long time
Never thought freedom would be mine

I can almost taste it
Touch it
Feel it
Burning deep inside of me
A strength I never knew
Strength to leave you

Written June 2001

September 11, 2001

"A day that will live in infamy"
I will never forget September 11th
Like my mother cannot forget
President Kennedy's assassination
Or the old-timers cannot forget
The beginning of the Great War

It will be a day forever branded
In our History books
In American schools our children will learn
The pride and prejudice we are ashamed of
And the beauty of the American Dream

No, I cannot, will not forget
For in forgetting our past
How can we learn from it?
How can we fight our fears
If we are unwitting slaves to them?

Our children will learn
Of our misguided anger
Towards Muslim Americans
"because they look the same"
As the ones who attacked our country

Our children will learn
Of Osama bin Laden
The man who orchestrated the attacks

Of his arrogance and fanaticism
Mistakenly believing
That our country would fall
And beg for mercy

We are Americans! we do not beg
We have never lost a war
We will fight back if we must
As we have so many times before
President Bush and General Powell
Are the only ones
Who need to do any talking now

Many lives will be lost
Many innocents will die in both countries
As many innocents died in the destruction
Of the World Trade Center
And the Pentagon

Over seven thousand lives were lost
Five planes were hijacked
All five are now accounted for
I remember hearing one crashed
In a rural area in Pennsylvania
Manned by brave passengers
Who fought back against the hijackers
And sacrificed their lives to save others

Two planes slammed into the Twin Towers
One closer to the base of one tower
The other higher up on the second tower

Another plane hit the Pentagon
The seat of our national security
I never heard
What happened to the fifth plane
Only that they found it

I heard of people who committed suicide
When they heard their loved ones were dead
I sympathize
I know what it's like
To want to get rid of the pain so badly
You can taste it

I've been there and back
I hadn't spoken about it to anyone
Not even in my writings
Until that news prompted me
To reveal everything to my mom

She's a wonderful, caring person
And I love her dearly
She held me as I cried
Just as she had when I was little
When I fell off my bike

I wept for my own lost soul
For the incredible loss of life
For many things
Some nameless fears

I used to write to take away my pain

Now I write to reveal it
I have laid my soul bare
To all of you now

I am just like you
I have joys, fears, anger
Like you, I experience regret
At what should've, could've, would've
Might've been

We are all the same on the inside
Each and every one of us
Throughout the world
We are all misguided, lost souls
Angels who have yet to earn their wings

Or maybe we are fallen angels
Who long for the glory of Heaven
Who long for peace
To reign on this war-weary planet

Maybe the tragedy was a warning
Not of a future attack
On our American Pride
But from God to take life
As it comes to us
To live for today
Instead of waiting for tomorrow
"because tomorrow's ground
Is too uncertain for plans"

Carpe diem, my friends. Carpe diem.

Written October 2001

Utopia (I Had a Dream)

I had a dream
That one day soldiers would throw down sword and shield
And take up their plows and farm the land
I had a dream
That the scientists who create nuclear weaponry
Will join the surge toward space
I had a dream
That the racists who believe only whites deserve to live
Will sit down and eat with minorities
I had a dream
That the hate crimes and abuse of the world
Would be no more

Why can't we see
That change needs to be
Heart-felt in the minds of
All peoples - it's something I dream of

This is my dream
For the future
For the children
For the sake of humanity
For all who are
For all who will be
For all who were
For all people
This is my dream

I had a dream
That drugs being sold in school playgrounds
Would give way to untainted sweets
I had a dream
That the unfortunate souls who spend their lives in poverty
Will live as kings

Why can't we see
Love can turn this world around
No matter what people say
I will always pray
That peace will reign
And love will conquer all

Written February 2000

The Faithful One

"Lord, when do I get what I want?" says the one filled with
greed.
"Money is the root of all evil," replies God solemnly.
"When can I have what I need?" asks another, with anguish.
"Not yet, child," says Yahweh, "I will eventually do what
you wish."
"I want it now!" cries the selfish one.
"I'm no patron of demands," replies the Eternal One.
"Lord, give me the strength," the weakened one says,
"To get through each and every day."
"You possess this already," He replies.
"Your strength already lives inside."
"Praise the Lord God Almighty!" shouts the faithful one
with voice and soul.
"You please Me," says the good Lord, "for My glorification
is your goal.
Though you suffer every day
You find the strength to say
'Praise He who rules Heaven and Earth!'
This is the judge of a person's worth
Not he who begs for My care
That has made others suffer, there
Will be no glory forevermore.
But the person who has worked for
Others to be clothed and fed
Instead of reciting words well read.
And he who praises Me
Shall find eternal glory."

So take these words deep inside your heart
And do your best to do your part.
Be charitable to one and all
And praise the Creator of all.

Written June 1997

Cats

Hundreds of cats,
Each one different.
Zillions of cats,
Taking a ball, spinning it.

Written February 1995

Untitled (Beatnik Parody)

I feel the nose hairs in my brain
Chocolate in my mind
Dancing aliens doing the tango
Stuff my mouth with garlic
Prism light burning
Cosignatory is my favourite word
Toilet papered trees
Gigabytes of random access memory
Purple Haze kicks ass

Written February 2002

I Wanna Be Like Britney Spears...

I wanna be like Britney Spears
That damn bitch has everything
I wanna sing like Christina Aguilera or Mariah Carey
So I can break glass wherever I go
I wanna look like a supermodel and dress like a slut
So I can finally get laid
I wanna be in one of those boy bands
So I can be the only member who really is a girl
I wanna be a popstar
So I can make people vomit
From the constant repetition of my songs
Yeah
I wanna be a real-life Barbie
'Cos I want everything!

Written February 2002

Ode to a Whale Shark

Serene as you can be
Whale shark, you have a ton of hosts
They crawl on you
But you don't mind it most

You're a quiet as can be
Whale shark, you never worry me
You are a fine sight to see
But please don't marry me

Written March 1997

Valentine's Knight

My handsome Knight, today is the day for love
I'd be your Queen of Hearts for the occasion
Or your Damsel waiting in the tower above

What would you like our special song to be?
Is it Celine Dion "all the way"
Or Paul McCartney singing "silly love songs" to me?

On the stereo put Barry White or Marvin Gaye
Give me a bouquet of roses
And we can dance the night away

Serenade me under the silvery moon
Or propose to me on the banks of the Seine
The time and place is up to you
Just don't let the romance ever end

Written February 2001

The Marriage Rite

Man:
I am yours
And you are mine
Our hearts are bound
Till the end of time

Woman:
I give myself to you
As you give yourself to me
Faithful and true
Is how we'll always be

Man:
I will stand by you
I will keep you from harm
I will be your shelter
Through any storm

Woman:
I'll enfold your heart in mine
I'll stand by your side
I will give you strength
And guide you to the light

Man:
I will hold you close
And comfort your fears
I will dry your eyes

When you shed your tears

Woman:
I will calm your anger
And your wants I will please
Sadness I'll erase
And pain I will cease

Both:
And though time may pass
And turn the sky to gray
Our love will last
Till the end of our days

Written February 2001

"Bless Me, Ultima" Haikus

Antonio's friend
Ultima knows everything
In his little heart

Tenorio's girls
Cursed Antonio's uncle
Ultima cures him

Tenorio kills
Ultima's owl and she dies
Antonio mourns

Ultima
A curandera
Collected herbs

Ultima
Was a witch
Accused of evil doings

Antonio
Friend to Ultima
Seven years old

The owl
Ultima's spirit
Tenorio shot it

Ultima died
When the owl died
Antonio mourned

Tenorio
People kicked him out of town
The end

Written February 2001

Cerberus

I stand before the gate that I once walked through
Into this world of darkness
The side on which I stand is carefully guarded by
The creature known as Cerberus

It is a creature not of physical manifestation
Of light or darkness bent
But of pain, guilt, sadness, lust, anger
And all the tears I've spent

Three huge heads stare at me with piercing black eyes
A hedge of wolf fangs warn me away
From the metallic gate which beckons me to pass through
And yet it bars my way

On the other side mortality waits patiently
For me to pass through
As I sit in front of both monster and gate
Unsure of what to do

I agonize and fantasize of passing
Through the gate
Abandoning this incessant darkness
An existence which I hate

For centuries I haven't seen the sun
Or held a woman in my arms
I've never known the joy of child-rearing

Of keeping <u>my</u> family from harm

An ancient specter mocks my attempts
To pass through the gate
"Give up this struggle - you can never return
To mortality - for that it's a little late!"

Another spirit on the other side encourages
Me to pass through
"It is a life which you've come to despise
And no longer meant for you"

"There is a way you can change what you are
I have faith that you can
You can return to a mortal, human life
And live and love as a man"

Maybe someday I'll pass through that gate
And leave this existence behind
But I know in the time between now and then
I won't get the thought out of my mind

Written April 2002

I Close My Eyes

It's been some time since we were together
As I gaze at the cards, I can still hear words of forever
The sound of your voice echoing in my ears
The twist in my heart as my eyes fill with tears
It took so long to figure out the reasons why
But that knowledge can't stop the tears I cry
I don't know why I keep holding on
When I know that I have to move on

Then I close my eyes
And I remember
All the late night calls and long talks
The day we strolled on the boardwalk
I close my eyes
And I remember
It was more than just a game to me
But things are never what they seem

And so I sit in the sun with the wind in my hair
Writing and wishing you were still here to care
But though you say you still want to be friends
That's something I know I just can't pretend
And my words can't change your point of view
But I know deep down you feel the same as I do
And so I continue to cry these tears
Even though it's been at least a year

'Cos I close my eyes

And I remember
The sensation of your lips against mine
And the feeling we were running out of time
I close my eyes
And I remember
When we first met how time stood still
I have ever loved you and always will

And I close my eyes...

I wonder how I can make it through
When every step I take leads me back to you

I close my eyes
And I remember
Every word you've ever said
And every tear I've ever shed
I just close my eyes
And I remember
The moment you walked away
How I long for those yesterdays

I close my eyes
And dream of you
I close my eyes
And I remember
You never kissed me goodbye

Written April 2004

All I Need

Late at night when I close my eyes
I need your touch 'cos it feels so right
When we're together, I look in your eyes
I see love and a promise of forever

Others promised the moon and stars
And left, taking with them a piece of my heart
I'm tired of being played for a fool
I'd give anything for someone true

Baby please stay
I don't ever want to let you go
Honey you know I love you
And I'll never let you go no
'Cos you're all I'll ever need

Written March 2000

Don't Know Why

I don't know why I feel the way I do
I spend every waking moment thinking of you
Honey there ain't no way around it, it's love that I feel
I can't get enough of your touch 'cos the feeling's oh so right
And I can't get enough of the way you make me feel
Boy I need you with me day and night

I don't know why I love you so
All I know is that I can't let you go
Baby you know I love you, there ain't no one else
I'll never need anyone else in my life but you baby
I want you for no one but myself
Boy your love makes me crazy

Too much is never enough
Don't you know that it's you I trust
And every night I thank the heavens above
Because I'm lucky enough to know your love
There's no one else I'm ever gonna need
I just need you right here with me

Written August 2001

Love is Over

Walking on the beach
Soft sand beneath bare feet
My life replays in my head
Memories bittersweet
As light fades to darkness
Memories still play in my mind
I can't bear the thought
Of leaving you behind

Staring at the stars
Wishing you were here to hold me
But I've slowly come to realize
It was never meant to be
The wind howls in dispair
The sound chills my heart
Why couldn't I keep us
From falling apart

Walking down the street
I see you ahead of me
My heart skips a beat
But you just pass by me
It was only a second
But it felt like an eternity
For the first time in ages
You turned and looked at me

We had an eternity before us

A lifetime ahead of us
But what stopped us
From being together forever
Now I'm alone in the dark
Hearing only the beat of my heart
Wishing I could reignite the spark
But our love is over

How did we lose the feeling now
It's gone and my heart only aches
And I'm alone wondering how
It got too strong for us to take
Maybe we can start over
Maybe not all is lost
But if it's really over
You'll still be in my heart

Written February 2000

Don't Walk Away

You say that you really love me
And that you're always thinking of me
Then why were you with her last night
Baby it just ain't right
Don't you know that I love you
And that I've been thinking of you
Why've you been cheating on me
Baby can't you see...

That I don't wanna lose you, don't wanna lose you
Don't wanna lose you 'cos I love you so
And even though you've hurt me, I still love you

So don't walk away
'Cos it's okay
Maybe we can try again
Maybe we can learn to love again
Please baby please
Just don't walk away

What I wanted is a real lover
But you're turning out like every other
You've put me through so much pain
But I'm willing to try again
Can't stand in the rain if you can't get wet
I can see dark clouds in the sky
Baby tell me why…

That you're leaving me, you're leaving me
Don't want you to leave 'cos I love you so
And even though you're far away, I still love you

So don't walk away
'Cos it's okay
Maybe we can try again
Maybe I can trust your heart again
Please baby please
Just don't walk away

You know, after all we've been through
I'm not about to give up on you
Not now, not yet
It's raining and I'm soaking wet
The sun will come after the rain
I can learn to trust your heart again
We can make it, together
Now and forever

I want you to be with me, want you to be with me
I want you to be with me 'cos I love you so
And even though I'm hurting, I still love you

So don't walk away
'Cos it's okay
Baby we can try again
I know the sun is gonna shine again
Please baby
Don't walk away

Written February 2000

The Road Home

I love you dearly, you know I do
I don't want anyone but you
But in your eyes, a pained soul's inside

I know what it's like to hide
Mask all the hurt you feel inside
But baby it just ain't right

You're just so alone - trying to find your way home
Why won't the pain ever end - alone, so alone
Just trying to find your way home
Trying to take the road home

I understand what it feels like
I've had troubles of my own to fight
Just trying to find my way home

I was just so alone - trying to find a way home
The pain doesn't wanna end - alone, so alone
Baby just trying to find the way home
Just trying to take the road home

Wanna take the road home baby
Take the road home—oh!
Get it over with baby....

Written October 1997

If You Only Knew

It's not that I can't live without you
It's just that I don't even wanna try
Baby you can't see how I feel about you
Baby I need you in my life

I'd pull down a star or two
Just for you
I'd do anything for you
Baby if you only knew

I don't know how it got so crazy
But I just want to set things right
All I'm ever gonna ask you for baby
Is to stay with me tonight

Just one night to be with you
Just you and me
I'll never give up on you
I just wanna be

With you for a lifetime
I just wanna be
All you ever need
The way I feel for you inside

But it's never gonna happen
It's only me
Oh it'll never ever happen

It's a dream that will never be

Written June 2001

Self-Absorbed

You say that you care
That you'll always be there
But you play me for a fool
And you don't go by the rules
I just want some affection
And a little attention
And something about honesty
Being the best policy
But you just lie to me
Why can't you see

That I just need a little love
I just need someone to care
I need someone
Who will always be there

When I was a little girl
I dreamed that somewhere in the world
There was a daddy for me
Who'd care for me
For so long, I held out hope
And now I'm at the end of my rope
'Cos you just turned and walked away
When all I wanted was for you to say

I'll give you a little love
I'll be someone who cares
I'll be someone

Who will always be there

Why is it everything I do
Is never good enough for you
Why does it hurt so bad
Make me sad, make me mad
Why don't you care
Why are you never there

All I want is a little love
All I need is someone to care
All I need is someone
Who's gonna be there

Yeah, all I want is love
I need someone to care
Yeah, I need someone
Who'll be there

All I need
All I need
Yeah, all I need
Is just a little love

You've got a lot of nerve
To say I'm self-absorbed
When all you did was
Use me like a dart board

All I wanted was a little love
All I needed was someone to care
It's too late now

'Cos you were never there

Written December 2001

Land of Enchantment

When I was young
The world as I knew it
Was a land of enchantment
But that's now gone
As I look at the news today
There's souls in enslavement

What's the matter
With everyone today
Why can't our problems
Just go away
I want to know
Why people are so cruel
It's something
I'll never get used to

The towers fell
Babylon the great whore
Laughs at the world's pain
The world's gone to hell
Like it never has before
But it will be there again

Why can't we learn
From history's mistakes
Recorded in the sands of time
That some give, some take
Why can't we be

Better than we were before
Why can't we try
To let peace reign once more

People are dying
People are crying
Why can't we take time
To let it be fixed
Why are blacks and whites
Forbidden to mix

We can do so much better
Than we did yesterday
But because everyone's selfish
The pain won't go away
I want to know
Why others get abused
Some use drugs
And others get used

Maybe one day
Things will get better
I hope and pray
As I write this letter
That people
Will begin to see
That we all need each other
To make it to eternity

Written February 2002

Leave Me Alone

Once I thought I loved you
And I wanted you to love me
I would have done anything for you
But you just couldn't see
You hurt me like I knew you would
I gave you all I could
But you didn't care and it hurt so bad
When I thought about what we once had

Once I would have believed
That you were the right one for me
If I only could have foreseen
That you'd rip my heart out and leave
I found myself on my knees for you
Just to get a little love out of you
Illusion is reality, reality is illusion
You put me in a constant state of confusion

I've had enough of you
Being with you
Changed my point of view
Just leave me alone now
Don't wonder how
I'll make it without you now

Things are different now
I'm stronger now
My heart no longer aches

My love you won't again take
I may have my head in the clouds
But I've got my feet on the ground
And I feel so much stronger
Now that you're not around

Written February 2002

You Don't Know Me

We've been together for such a long, long time
But there's something I've got on my mind
We don't hang together the way we did anymore
We don't do things together the way we did before
We used to make love morning, noon or night
Now all we ever do is scream and fight
I wish I could go back to the way it used to be
But now it seems that you never really knew me

It used to be all good
Now nothing's the same
You don't know me like you did
'Cos everything's changed
I gave you what I had to give
But I can't give no more
You don't love me like you did
Anymore....

I wish I could change our affair's circumstances
But now I've got to take a chance on new romances
It ain't easy for me to let our relationship go
But I've come to realize you don't want me no more
What happened to us - we used to be tight
Now it seems I can't do nothing right
I wish I could take back the moment I first knew
You'd be in my life, 'cos I never really knew you

It used to be all good

But nothing's the same
You don't know me like you did
Now you can't remember my name
I loved you for free
And never asked for more
But you'd rather go with some
Cheap whore

If only I could turn back the hands of time
Then you never would have been mine
'Cos I don't want to spend my life waiting for you
To come around when I could be seeing somebody new

Written February 2002

Don't Leave Me Now

I didn't mean to hurt you
Baby I was so wrong
How could I refuse to believe
That you were right all along
I didn't mean to hurt you
Didn't mean to make you cry
Baby I'm so sorry
Please just try

To forgive me
For what I put you through
But you know
It hurts me too

I don't want you to cry
Baby it'd make me so blue
To know that your leaving
Is because I hurt you
I didn't mean what I said
I was so wrong to say
That it was over between us
I wish I could take those words away

Please forgive me
For everything I put you through
But don't you know
That it hurts me too

Baby I'm sorry - please stay
Baby don't take your love away
'Cos I need you by my side
Give our love one more try
How could I lose you now
All I ask
Is don't leave me now

If I could take back
Everything I said
I'd start over again
I'd make you forget
The hurt I put you through
I'm so sorry - you know I love you

Written February 2002

Daddy's Little Girl

It seems that some kids are just born lucky
Where did all my good luck run off to
Never had a strong hand to keep me steady
And as for happy moments I've had so few
No one seems to understand my pain
Or why there are tears in my eyes
I wish someone was here to wipe them away

I always wanted to be
Daddy's little girl
But the harsh reality of the unloved
Was my whole world
Where was my protector
My comfort, my solitude, my safety
Time closed that door
And I almost went crazy
Now I realize
Out there's a whole new world
But deep inside I still want to be
Daddy's little girl

The long journey took a lot out of me
And for a while I couldn't go on
The helping angels arriving I couldn't see
All my hope, my joie de vivre was gone
But time has changed me, opened up my eyes
Although I hurt, I've been created anew
And the grace of the Lord made me realize

That there's a heavenly Father
And I'm His little girl
Now I feel His love
And it's changed my world
In Him there's my protection
My comfort, my solitude, my safety
I've returned to the fold
And found what was missing within me
And now I know
That out there's a whole new world
But I wish a mortal man could be
A daddy to this little girl

There's so much I still don't know
There's such pain - it's hard to let go
Through the tears it gets hard to see
But I know that eventually
My faith will be restored
I won't be alone anymore
And I know, oh I know...

That I'll never be
My daddy's little girl
But the pain of it no longer
Destroys my fragile world
Although he'll never be there
To walk me down the aisle
I know that when my life is over
I'll be greeted by the Father's smile
Oh I know

That there's a love for me in this world
And my own daughter will be
Her daddy's little girl

Written June 2002

Beautiful

Sometimes the world can bring you down
And the road seems so long
Feeling lost with no hope to be found
And you're so all alone
Sometimes the world seems to own you
People comment on everything you do
They don't understand what you're going through
And they don't really know you
But no matter what they say
You are beautiful in every way
And they can't take that away

You are beautiful
Though sometimes it's hard to see
You are beautiful
Because you are all that you can be
And I know
That it doesn't always seem that way
But just look in the mirror and say
"I am beautiful"

Sometimes it seems like nothing will change
That time is standing still
It seems that no one can find the dreams they claim
Because of a lack of will
But it's perfectly fine to have your head in the clouds
So long as your feet are on the ground
Though the harsh world can make you want to shout aloud

Nothing can keep you down
So just follow your dreams
No matter how tough it seems
And one day you will see

You are beautiful
Though sometimes it's hard to believe
You are beautiful
Even though it's sometimes hard to see
Don't you know
You are worth more than silver or gold
And it's only right that you should know
You are beautiful

Maybe someday the world will understand
That no one has the right to judge any woman or man
And maybe someday the rest of the world will believe
In the beauty that lies in you that I can see

Written August 2002

Faithfully Yours

You know truthfully baby
That you mean the world to me
And all I want is you baby
I'm fascinated by all you do
You say you want a love that's real
All you gotta do is prove how you feel
'Cos if we're gonna be together
It's gotta be forever

You're my sunlight in my day
You're the rainbow in my rain
In my fire, you're my flame
You're the engine to my train
All I'll ever need is you
For you, there's nothing I won't do
And I know it will last forever
'Cos we'll always be together

And there's no disguising
Ooh that my temperature's rising
With everything that you do
I'm so amazed by you

Baby, I'm faithfully yours
And don't ever ask for more
I'll stand by you, for sure
I'm faithfully yours
You'll never be alone

In me you'll find a home
I'm faithfully yours
Time is on our side
So you'll never have to hide it
I'm faithfully yours
Like it's from the stars above
That's the power of our love

Written August 2002

All I Know

Don't ask me why I feel this way
'Cos I can hardly understand it
And you're so far away
But I just have to deal with it

You may not understand why
Why I'm not with another man
Or the tears I cry
When my feelings are more than I can stand

I feel more deeply for you than I can show
I love you with a strength I've never known
But now your love is all I know
And I'm in too deep to let you go

There's no way I can begin to describe it
The love I feel for you
The empty space in my heart has been filled
Gone is the loneliness I once knew

L'amour de toi et moi c'est tout
Une emotion de nous
De ton coeur et mon coeur
Maintenant nous vivrons au bonheur
Mon tresor, mon amour
C'est vraiment l'amour
Et je t'aimerai toujours

There's no way I can begin to describe it
The love I feel for you
But now your love is all I know
And I'm in too deep to let you go

I'm in deep
And I can't let you go

Written March 2003

Love is All

"If I speak in human and angelic tongues but do not have love, I am a resounding gong or a clashing cymbal. And if I have the gift of prophecy and comprehend all mysteries and all knowledge; if I have all faith so as to move mountains but do not have love, I am nothing. If I give away everything I own, and if I hand my body over so that I may boast but do not have love, I gain nothing.
Love is patient, love is kind. It is not jealous, [love] is not pompous, it is not inflated, it is not rude, it does not seek its own interests, it is not quick-tempered, it does not brood over injury, it does not rejoice over wrongdoing but rejoices with the truth. It bears all things, believes all things, hopes all things, endures all things."
- 1 Corinthians 13, KJV

Some people think that love is just a plaything
That you can toy with then throw away at will
Some think that love is an insatiable hunger
A bottomless void longing to be filled
And though the philosophers discuss it
They hardly seem to know themselves
But real love is the greatest miracle
It just isn't something you put away on a shelf
It's the rarest of gifts given to us
It's not just a mere emotion, it's far more
Than any of us could ever dream of
And it's about time that that the world know...

That love is all
To everything and everyone
Love is all
That you need to show someone

It's in a word, in a touch
And it can mean oh so much
To a woman, child or man
Love is all
That you need, that you can

Some people spend their whole lives searching
In tiny villages and crowded cities for love
But they don't realize that this precious gift
Is sent straight to them from above
It's not in factories, aged trees or ancient ruins
It's right in the midst of their lives

Love is all
To the weak and the strong
Love is all
Whether it feels right or wrong
It's in a hug, in a smile
And there's no need to travel miles
It's always right here
Love is always
In your heart

When your life is over
When it all has come to an end
You'll know you had the chance to love
And you won't have that chance again

In a word or a touch
And it means so much
In a hug or a smile

No need to travel miles
Love is always right here
In your heart

Yes it is right here
In your heart

Written September 2002

Dance with Me

Get this party going on
Move to the rhythm all night long
Just get up out of your seat
Relax and get lost in the beat
Let the sound take you away
From midnight till the break of day
Leave behind your cares
Throw your hands in the air

Now everybody's feeling fine
One more dance and you'll be mine
Take you to another state of mind
Just leave your worries behind
All your troubles will float away
If you decide to stay
Come on and dance with me tonight
I wanna dance with you till the morning light

Let the music make you free
Just get on the floor
And dance with me
Let the music take control
Get on up and feel the groove
Surrender to the beat

Can you feel the groove
Just feel the rhythm
And dance with me

Gotta let your body move
Gotta make it strong
Let it move your feet

Let the music take control
Let it wash over you
Feel it in your soul
Just listen to the sound
When the music takes you
You will finally have found

Let it ease your mind
Leave your cares behind
Let it free your mind
Let it free your soul
You'll never let it go
Deep in your soul
If you wanna get away
From midnight to the day
It will take you away

Just shake it baby
Move it to the music
You'll escape
When you get a hold of it
Can't deny that it feels right
Leave it going on tonight

Written September 2002

No Greater Love

"There is no greater love than this, to lay down one's life for one's friends." - *John 15:13, NRSV*

A hero is a rare breed of man
He does whatever he can
To help whoever is in need
Those who are trapped, he frees
For those who are weak, he is strong
He judges no man, right or wrong
Everyday he risks his life
To heal pain and strife
And though he asks for nothing
To those he helps, it means something
To them he's an angel from above
For there is no greater love

A mother will sacrifice everything
So that her children will know no pain
She gives them what she was denied
While burying her own dreams deep inside
She finds them when they stray
When they fall, she wipes their tears away
She teaches them all that she knows
And when the time comes, she lets them go
When she is old, her grown children
Will care for her like she did for them
To them she's an angel from above
For there is no greater love

We are who we are today
Because earthly angels guided our way
And when we help, asking for nothing in return
We will learn
What it is to truly love
One day we will know
That there's no greater love

Written September 2002

A Little Bit of Love

Never had I imagined
That love would feel like this
Never thought I'd feel such passion
That my life would change with a kiss
And when I'm down and lonely
You're right here by my side
My love is like an ocean
My feelings I just cannot hide

When I'm hurt and my pride is broken
You're here to comfort me
When the world's caved in on me again
Your love's all I need
You quiet that voice inside my head
That tells me I'm not good enough
You calm the storms that rage in me
When life becomes too tough

I need a man with the strength everyday
To move the mountains that stand in my way
I need a man who'll take me to a better place
And stand by me no matter what I face
Someone who'll calm my fears and dry my tears
So I won't be alone or afraid
Someone who knows what to do to ease my pain
And show me how to live again
And that's just what I get when I'm with you
I wanna give you so much in return

Everyday I learn
That there's nothing I won't do for you
'Cos through the dark times, you helped me through

I don't have to face another day of pain
The sunlight has come after the rain
Just like I always knew it would
You've done for me more than anyone could
I know in my heart, we all have a cross to bear
What makes it easier is knowing someone cares
When my confidence is on shaky ground
You lift my spirits and turn it all around
I just call your name and you're there
You're the answer to all my prayers
Through the storm, through the night
Your presence makes it all right
I belong to you, heart and soul
And I'm never gonna let you go
In you, I've found the truth and the way
'Cos of you, I'm standing in the light of day
All I need is you to hold me and to love me
Let me know you're thinking of me
And my worries shall be erased
In you, I've found a brighter place
When the morning comes I'm good as new
And I take this night I've shared with you
With me, and I smile when I think of you
No matter what at that moment I may do
Your smile shines on me like the sun
And now I know it's only just begun
Baby I'll always believe in you

And I know we'll see this through
I know I don't have to hide
'Cos true love is on my side
And that's the love that I can claim
Baby, when you call my name

Something's catching fire
You're love takes me higher
I've done it before and I'll do it again
If you pick me up, I can jump right back in
Your love gives me the power
I'm getting stronger by the hour
There's no doubt about it, you see
I truly do believe
That I just have to see what you can do
And then I can do it too
Baby at the end of the day
A little love goes a long way

Just a little bit of love
Is all I need
Someone to take care of me
When troubles seem too deep
Just a little bit of love
Is all I really need
Someone who'll be there for me
Someone who'll care for me
A little love's all I need
And that's what I can claim
Baby when you call my name

A little bit of love
Is all I'll ever need
Words just aren't good enough
To prove the depth of your love
A little bit of love
Is all I need
To make all my anger cease
And to give me a sense of release
A little love's all I need
And that's the love I can claim
Baby when you call my name

Love can free your mind now
And it can free your soul

Written September 2002

Fourth of July

Too early in life I had given up hope
That love would be mine
But I was reborn when I met you
On the Fourth of July
Who would've believed I'd fall in love
All over again
Who could've known that in you I'd find
A love that would never end
And my life was clear, I began to live again
You're where I belong forever

A year after we had first met
On that same summer night
Sitting close enough to just barely touch
In the twilight
Then we wandered away to a secret place
Where we could hide
So no one could see us or at least
We could pretend
Young lovers laughing and holding hands
Underneath the stars

Fireworks went off in the darkened sky
Making colourful designs
And as you kissed me, I got butterflies
Trembled inside
Left the world behind as roman candles
Soared above the park

You held me tightly as I pressed against you
There in the dark
And we ignited a different spark
I lost my heart to you

Suddenly we lay together on the grass
I felt a little shy
But breathless, fervid and flush with desire
Amid dandelions and fireflies
It swept over me like the wind in the trees
At your blissful sigh
Delicately lay entwined, tangled up
And on a natural high
Drifting to another state of mind
Floating away

Left reality and the rest of the world behind
At least for a short while
So beautiful and bittersweetly we melded together
But time went sailing by
Thunderclouds hovered threatening to pour
Then the rain began to fall
I wanted to stay but didn't want to get wet
We hid 'neath trees so tall
Then ran to my house as the rain continued to fall
With a warm gentle breeze

The feeling I had with you
Had been so heady and sublime
But we had to leave our secret place
So far behind

We had to go our separate ways
We gave each other a reluctant good-bye
And I got weak in the knees
As you tentatively kissed me good-night

The rain stopped and a crescent moon shone
As I lay in bed that night
I realized that everything I knew about love
Had been far from right
When we came together and let love lead the way
I knew I was yours and you were mine
No other day in my life has been so magical
As that Fourth of July
Now I eagerly await for us to celebrate
Another Fourth of July

Written November 2002

Through the Fire

I was caught in the pouring rain with nowhere to run
Feeling alone and confused without anyone
I felt like the world around me had shattered
I was distraught, broken, burned, torn and tattered
I was crying out for someone to save me
But nobody came into my life and I was so lonely
Shadows of distant memories began to hem me in
But I found strength in my faith and from within

There is so much more I have yet to learn
But when darkness falls, I know where I can turn
To the One who created me with His own hands
When they say I can't pull through, I know I can
I'll just keep going, holding on steadfastly
And His grace shines on me and sets me free
Though I've been hurt a lot, I still know how to love
'Cos of the strength that came down to me from above

There'll be times in your life when you fall
But know that His love for you can conquer it all
And His grace will keep you safe
Will guard you with every precious breath you take
When the cold wind blows, don't hesitate or give in
You have everything you need within Him
Don't ever put your good heart away on a shelf
Just look inside, keep praying and saying to yourself

I can make it through the fire and the rain

Just as long as I believe anything is possible
I'll be able to stand tall, on my own once again
And I know that the hard times made me stronger
And in time my broken heart will mend
Lord, I know I don't have to be scared
'Cos I know You're always there
And I know despite all the sorrow and pain
I'll be able to make it through the fire and the rain

When there's no end in sight
And your dreams seem so far away
When you're lost in the night
You'll find your home in the light of day
When you feel inferior inside
Or feel so out of place
Know you have nothing to hide
And there's nothing you can't face

You'll make it through the fire and the rain
If you put your cares in His hands, all is possible
You'll be able to stand on your own two feet again
Know that the hard times will only make you stronger
And in time your wounded heart will mend
Through all the thunder and lightening of the storm
You'll never come to any harm
With His peace and strength, you can climb the highest wall
He'll give you hope when it seems you've lost it all
You'll never have to be scared
'Cos the Lord is always there
You're not alone, it's ok
You'll make it one more day

Despite all the sorrow and the pain
You're gonna make it through the fire and the rain

You'll be safe and sound
Hang onto the faith you've found
In times of need
All you gotta do is believe
When hurt or poverty strikes
Know you'll make it through the night
If you've been stigmatized
Whether you're black or white
Regardless of what side of life
He'll heal your pain and strife
And you'll see the world's beauty
And say thank You for delivering me

Written December 2002

Twisted Lullaby

Here's a story
About a little girl
Who became a woman
A look inside her world
At what she had to learn

Let's flashback a few years
Talk about childhood fears
A girl hiding, crying in her room
Hoping the pain'll be over soon
Turns on the radio to her favourite songs
Trying to escape the hurt as she sings along
Tears in her eyes, rage in her heart
Trying to keep herself from falling apart
And as the sun sinks in the sky
The night brings a twisted lullaby

The pain never ends
It briefly fades
Then returns to taunt her again

Let's take it back to the beginning
When she hardly had begun living
A child in her mama's arms
An innocent vulnerable to the harm
That would come the moment her father leaves
Her little heart breaking in grief
Her tiny soul weeping

Her infant voice screaming
And as her father walks away into the night
The wind sighs in a twisted lullaby

It's impossible to forget
When from the beginning
She's never felt loved, only felt pain

Let's take it forward now to a few years before
The perfect student with the perfect score
Collapsing under the weight of her pain
Hiding the truth, her reality, in shame
Her grades suffer and she feels like a failure
Taking the blame for everything that ails her
Staring at her reflection, hating what she sees
But I bet you didn't realize this girl is.... me
But I'm still alive and keep carrying on
And the twisted lullaby becomes my song

Don't assume you know
The story behind someone's eyes
We all have pain we hide deep inside

And the twisted lullaby becomes my song
I'll keep carrying on
Singing my song

Written January 2003

Love (That Lasts A Lifetime)

The day I met you I was a little scared
I was so very unprepared
For when you'd break down my defenses
The walls began to tumble down
And everytime I looked around
There you were, right by my side

I never really knew what love was like
Could never trust or open up
I'd always hide my feelings inside
But when I met you, deep down I knew

This could be the love that lasts a lifetime
The love that lasts my whole life through
I want to always be by your side
And live forever and a day with you

Time passes far too slowly for me
I just can't wait to see
You, for the first time, right in front of me

There's nothing I can hide from you
I just can't fight this feeling
And I'm never ever gonna give up on you
I love you, and I know you feel the way I do

This could be the love that lasts a lifetime
The love that lasts our whole lives through

I know I'll always be by your side
And spend the rest of my life with you

Every song I hear reminds me of you
Every night I long to be close you
This distance I hate
I can no longer wait
I just want to spend my life with you

Written March 2003

Rainbow

I was so scared and sad
Love I never had
Abandoned by my own dad
I thought that to love someone
had to give till it was gone
But not anymore

I once lived in sadness
In madness
Forgot the meaning of gladness
Darkness surrounded me
I needed to be free
And be myself again

Never had I imagined
I'd ever fit in
Or that there'd be a fight I'd win
But somehow it all changed
Nothing's the same
As it was before

They thought that if they'd forsake me
Loneliness would break me
And despondency would take me
But I'm far from finished yet
Against me you can never bet
'Cos you'll never win

The storm and darkness is gone
And I know I'm not alone...

And I see the rainbow

Written March 2002

Ma Vie

Le temps passant dans ma vie
Je n'ai pas peur
Car j'peux voir des jours d'bonheur
Je sais mon âme est vrai
J'ai le pouvoir d'aimer
J'ai la force d'un vainqueur
Dans mon coeur

J'aime et j'ai la haine aussi
J'ai ri et j'ai pleuré
Mais somme toute je survivrai
Je sais mon âme est vrai
J'ai le pouvoir d'aimer
J'ai la force d'un vainqueur
Dans mon coeur

Je sais le chemin et froid
Et ce n'est toujours pas clair
Quelle chance
Que c'est je sais les choix
De la paix et de la guerre
De ma vie

Written July 2002

I'll Love Again (Things Have Changed)

What's been going on
Time has passed so quickly
Things aren't the way they used to be
You're so different now
I don't understand how
You could be so indifferent to me
If you decide to leave me
I know that I gave you the best of me

Tell me why you're silent
You don't call me on the phone
And you ignore me all the time
The illusion is gone
That what we had would last
If it ends, I know that I'll still be fine
If you ever decide to leave
I know I gave you all the best of me

Whenever you needed me
I was always there
But if I mean nothing to you
Then it wouldn't be fair

Things have changed between us
And if what we had has come to an end
I know I'll love again
Things have changed between us
If it's over I know I'll be okay

'Cos I'll love again

Written July 2002

I Will Sing

When the spotlight dims and the glitter fades
When it's all a memory
After the dreams inside my head
Have become reality
When there's no one to hear my songs
And to murmur or sing along

When my children have come to be
And time turns my hair to grey
When I've made a house a home
And they're old enough to fly away
When the nest I've built is empty
Save for me and a box of memories

When my children have children of their own
And I've become too frail to walk
When I'm nearing the end of of my life
And I'm lucky I can still talk
I'll carry my song, my music, my art
Deep inside my heart

I will sing
I will sing
I will sing
I will sing always

And I will love you
Yes, I will love you

I'll always love you
My love will never fade

We make choices in this life
That can lead to failure or victory
But regardless, we must appreciate it
Because it's so fleeting

Written February 2003

Love Survives

There's indecision and confusion within me
But I'd give anything to make you see
That I just wanna be with you
The nights are getting longer
And loneliness is getting stronger
What more can I do?
If only you'd tell me that you love me
Instead of answering with silence
Then I could be sure of how you feel
If I hear those words on your lips

Now so much time has passed us by
Yet you're still here by my side
Now I know you love me for sure
It doesn't matter if it's right or wrong
When the emotions feel so strong
I could not love you more
I always will love you
Please understand
I will never desert you
As long as you're my man

Even in the darkest hour
No matter what the cost
With love's great power
No soul can be lost

When

You're lying beside me
There's no doubt in my mind
That love survives
I know that love survives

Written August 2002

How Much Would it Take

I don't understand how
How you could be so blind
To not notice that I feel
Like I'm losing my mind

I don't understand how
How you could be so cold
I can't believe you don't love me
When you're all that I know

Tell me how much would it take
For you to love me - is there any way
That I can get to your heart
I don't want us to ever be apart
Tell me how much would it be
For you to see this love inside of me
My heart's about to break
Tell me how much would it take

It isn't fair at all
To love someone so deeply
To love someone so completely
When they don't seem to care

Tell me how much would it take
Tell me will there ever be a way
For me to always be with you
Please tell me what to do

Tell me will we ever be
The orchestra in love's symphony
I don't want my heart to break
Tell me how much would it take
What would it take

Written August 2002

Whortleberries

As I walked out one Sunday morn
To take a breath of fresh air
A young man I happened to meet
And thus he spoke to me fair
"Where you off to so early on?"
Said I - "to Kurkstan fell
To get some ripe whortleberries
But where you goin' yourself?"

He said nothing but he linked his arm
In mine, and off we went
Over many a stream and many a bog
And many a grassy bend
Where the sparrows on a furze-bush chirped
And the stonechats on a stone
And the sound of their strange call
Was "boy, kiss her now that you're alone"

He kissed me once, he kissed me twice
He kissed me twenty times
We then sat down on a boulder
And he recited an old love-rhyme
Of silken gowns and silver crowns
And other magicks that be
And I forgot the ripe whortleberries
As he brushed up against me

How blessed was I while in his arms

As he held me to his heart
He laid his cheek upon my hair
And vowed we'd never part
His dark blue eyes gazed into mine
And shone as bright as the sun
His embrace was strong and tender
And meant for me alone

I've wandered many a lonesome road
On fate's capricious wing
I spent many a time away in
Many a pleasurable spring
But the greatest day of my life
I've often told myself
Was spent gathering whortleberries
Down by Kurkstan fell

Do you have whortleberries
On the mountainside far away
Where fresh blooms shine in the sun
On the mountainside far away

Written August 2002

La Fin D'Amour

Dans mon coeur c'est une inquietude
Tu es trop distante de moi
Et mais c'est la fin de notre amour
Je ne peux pas vivrai sans toi
Ooh je ne veux être de nous
J'ai besoin de toi
Car je ne suis rien sans toi

Oh j'ai beaucoup de froid sans toi
C'était un accident
Que je t'aime de tout mon âme
Quand te ne m'aime
Donne-moi une chance, s'il te plait
Car sans toi
Je ne peux pas vivrai

A la nuit, je crie ton nom
Et le monde arrête sans toi
Car partout je te vois
Ma vie est rien sans toi
Tous les jours que j'ai pleuré
Je seul besoin de toi
Je t'aimerai toujours
Mais c'est la fin d'amour

Donne-moi une chance, s'il te plait
Car sans toi

Je ne peux pas vivrai

Written September 2002

Untitled (In The Boat)

A late summer breeze
gently nudges the small boats against the dock.
The waves quietly slap against their aged wooden hulls
carelessly as the seagulls cry in the distance.
The lateness of the day has a sense of freedom,
of letting go.

As I climb into my boat,
my troubles fade and my only thought
is of the warm sun shining down on me
and where the current will take me.

Perhaps I will sail past
the houses on the edge of the river
that loom like silent sentinels
guarding the waterfront
as if wary of a seaborne enemy.

Perhaps I will drop anchor,
and spend the last remaining daylight fishing,
or maybe just reading
one of the books I take with me when I travel,
these old friends that I know so well.

Then when the light begins to fade,
and twilight descends,
I will return to the docks
and tie it to the dock's postings,

then climb out and go home,
leaving my little boat waiting
in anticipation of another day.

Written September 2002

Ruminations

Please, kind sir.
Take pity on a weary traveler.
The night is getting colder,
and I have naught to wear but these rags.
I see your family,
basking in the warm glow of a well-stoked fire.
Can I not but sit before it for even a short time?

My heart is heavy,
and my burden weighs on my back.
My body is sore, and my soul is weary.
For I have traveled this road for so long,
and I have not yet been able to rest.

Why can I not throw my burden off, you ask?
Kind sir, I am so weary
that I no longer have the strength
to set it down myself.
My strength ebbs from me,
but I must shoulder my burden,
even as I sink to my knees and my back begins to break.

I am exhausted,
but I am forced to continue
down this endless road,
carrying my increasingly weighty burden.

What is my burden, you ask?

My memories.
My experiences.
My past.
My thoughts.
My dreams.
My regrets.
Is it any wonder that my burden is so heavy?

What is this road I travel?
It is called Life, my friend.
My journey has been a brief one
compared to the journeys of innumerable others.

In nomine Domini,
I ask that you let me stay,
if only for awhile.
I will be unnoticeable among you.
I promise I will not stay long,
for I have miles to go before I sleep.

Written December 2001

Untitled (Lord James Grey & Moonstone)

You are a source of love unconditional
Your contented purrs echo in the room
As I gently scratch under your chin
Your body brushes against my leg, soft hairs tickling
Your eyes widen at the sight of something interesting
And you make hungry little mews at the smell of food

You box with each other for dominance
Two children at play
You scale the mountains of boxes fearlessly
Even as they sway and threaten to topple

You peer eagerly out the window
Fascinated by the bitter cold world outside
From the safety of this room
You stretch regally on the bookcase
Bathed in sunlight

You are gifts from the divine
And what fortunate souls you are
To have been snatched from the jaws of death
And brought into a loving home just in time
I need nothing else than this
Your companionship to brighten my days
And warm my nights
As long as the fates allow

Written December 2005/Previously unreleased

Graffiti on my Bedroom Wall

I am not weak
I am strong
I am not a victim
I've survived it all
I will be a New York Times bestselling author
Because I'm that talented
I am beautiful
I am sexy
I am me

I am beautiful just as I am

Written throughout 2012/Transcribed February 2014

The Battle Hymn of Leah's Knights

Mine eyes have been subject to a most dreadful plight
An abomination in the form of a saga called Twilight
Yet, among the purple prose and misogynistic blight
Her Awesome marches on!

Leah, Leah, Leah Clearwater!
Leah, Leah, Leah Clearwater!
Leah, Leah, Leah Clearwater!
Her Awesome marches on!

I have seen her in the circle of Samuel Uley's pack
The wolf whose gleaming pelt doth match his heart of
charr'ed black
Yet, even as his subordinates do stab her in the back
Her Awesome marches on!

Leah, Leah, Leah Clearwater!
Leah, Leah, Leah Clearwater!
Leah, Leah, Leah Clearwater!
Her Awesome marches on!

In her quest for freedom, she hath joined the pack of Jacob
Because she is not welcome in Sam Uley's little club
Yet, even when she must take orders from a spoiled, whiny
cub
Her Awesome marches on!

Leah, Leah, Leah Clearwater!
Leah, Leah, Leah Clearwater!
Leah, Leah, Leah Clearwater!
Her Awesome marches on!

Such total hotness is unequaled among the Quileute tribe
Any sporker wisely knows she's better off with a diff'rent
scribe
And in our headcanon, she gives the packs a much-
deserv'ed diatribe
Her Awesome marches on!

Leah, Leah, Leah Clearwater!
Leah, Leah, Leah Clearwater!
Leah, Leah, Leah Clearwater!
Her Awesome marches on!

And so we pledge our troth to her, our Lady Wolf comrade
To defend her from the spars of a series so horrendously
bad
We'll throw a kegger for her, Emmett Cullen and Mustache
Dad!
Their Awesome will march on!

Leah, Leah, Leah Clearwater!
Leah, Leah, Leah Clearwater!
Leah, Leah, Leah Clearwater!
Her Awesome marches on!

Written March 2013

The ABC's of Anti-Twilight

A is for Aborted
What Edward demanded Renesmee be
B is for Boffing
The entire Cullen family tree

C is for Charlie
Whose mustache we like

D is for Demetri
Who only wishes he was Spike

E is for Edward
His emo makes us snore

F is for Faeries
What they should be named for

G is Goddamn
As in the hole in Bella's chest

H is for Headache
What we get when we read the rest

I is for Ignorant
For which Meyer has no excuse

J is for Jealous
What fans call us--they can't handle the truth

K is for Killing
When you want to, the Cullens hand you the key

L is for Larceny
How Alice got herself the car in Italy

M is for Money
Meyer's reason for publishing her wet dreams

N is for Nooooo!
When Book Four was split in two films, we screamed

O is for Oversexed
Bella's personality--if a bit on the nose

P is for Purple
The colour of Stephenie Meyer's prose

Q is for Questions
Seth won't let you ask her

R is for Romance
It's completely beyond Meyer

S is for Stupid
The entire series in a nutshell

T is for Trauma
Because the books put us through hell

U is for Umpire
The sparkly vampires play baseball

V is for Victorian
Because a bodice ripper would show it all

W is for Wasteful
The Cullen's spending is exactly it

X is for Xenophobia
Why the vamps give the wolves such shit

Y is for Yammer
The only thing the characters have done

Z is for Zero, zip
The letters left—I hope you liked this one!

Written July 2013

Shadeless Grey

You think you're just so very very smart
Pretending that your terrible porn is high art
But if your "hero" were completely broke
On your head there'd fall the joke
Because that young and nubile co-ed's smile
Would be staring out from a cold-case file

Your main man is an abusive jerk
And no, that's not how kinky sex works
Real people who've done that stuff before
Find your descriptions an unrealistic bore
You've built your wealth off of real-life misery
Saying that love is a cure-all for life's history
That a woman must learn to take pain for her man
And if she hates it, it's 'cause she doesn't understand

You think that getting laid can heal the patterns of abuse?
Well there's no school that can make you un-obtuse
That having sex means your love is undying?
My dear, it's to yourself and others you're lying
Real life simply doesn't work that way
There's fifty shades of difference 'tween abuse and play
But it doesn't matter what those who know better say
You're too busy counting your millions anyway

Written February 2015/Previously unreleased

Walk This Road

This was never how it was supposed to be
I realized that you're leaving today
Though I've lost you, you're still within
I hope you'll understand someday
My heart feels stronger when I'm with you
How was it that I lost my way?
Two souls can drift apart without a word
Were those the words I didn't say?

And we did not start out here, you and I
With our dreams in pieces on the ground
My soul is only half-alive without you
Things changed, and we lost what we'd found
As you wander off the path for an illusion
I'm lost in emptiness without a sound
I would walk this road again with you
If you would only just turn back around

How could you leave me in this despair?
Do you see the track of my every tear?
I am dragged down into a dark abyss
Only holding you will ease my fear
Only your love will soothe this pain
Stay with me, my love, be near
Come to me, show me that beauty
Too rich for use, for earth too dear

I once searched the world for one like you

And nothing else ever felt as right
As when we first took the chance we had
And through the dark, love shined a light
But the love has grown dim in your eyes
As you steadily fade out of sight
The loneliness swallows me whole
I don't know if I'll make it through the night

I disappear within, a shadow of myself
As the love dies, and it all falls away
For worse or better, I am bound to you
And those chips will fall where they may
Come back and give your love only to me
Don't fear the shadows along the way
I'd walk this road with you wherever it leads
If your heart would only come home to stay

Written December 2014/Previously unreleased

How Can I Be Silent?

How can I be silent when the world sings around me?
Life ebbs and flows with the waters of eternity
Dreams dredged up from the sea of Mind
Beauties unknown with no sense of space and time

This is what I heard in the world's every breath
A pulse, a beat, ever present, never stopping for death
The song of future, present and past together unwind
From deep within the deepest reaches of Universal Mind

A song of joy, sorrow, laughter and pain
A song of sea-salt air and bending fields of grain
A song of peace and war, of truth and lie
The song where there is new life as old ones die

The song is eternal, neverending, in everything I see
So I cannot be silent when the world sings to me

Written August 2015/Previously unreleased

Hymn of Gratitude to the Muses

Memory's Daughters
You have blessed me greatly
Full is my quiver of word-arrows
They fly on the breath of your consent

Calliope
Told to me the tale of my life
How wars could be fought
In the battlefield of my mind

Clio
Reminded me of my history
Shaking dust from hidden volumes
So I know where I came from

Erato
Reminded me of my passions
For life, for love, for understanding
So others may be understood

Euterpe
Taught me the right words
To say what needed to be said
And what can't be said any other way

Melpomene
Showed me that tears can be lovely
The saddest song can bring peace in its wake

But it must be sung to soothe

Polyhymnia
Let me glimpse the music of the spheres
Finding order within the chaos
Of the geometry of life

Terpsichore
Danced her dances with me
Showed me that all the beats of life
Move with muscle-memory

Thalia
Showed me how to find humour
Even amidst my darkest hours
Comedy being tragedy plus time

Urania
Showed me the heavens
Where the heights of my future lie
If I am brave enough to reach for it

And the song spins on
Through life and death
Height and breadth
Light and dark
Begins, ends
And begins again

Written August 2015/Previously unreleased

Want to read more by Melissa Treglia?
Visit her website:

www.melissatreglia.com

About the Author

Melissa Treglia lives in New Jersey with her mother, husband and three cats. She graduated from Brick Computer Science Institute in 2005 with a 3.6 GPA, after majoring in Web Design and Programming.

She's been making up stories from the time she first learned how to pick up a pencil and write her name. Her first short story was written by the age of five, and she published her first poem at fourteen. In 2015, she released the poetry collection *Apocryphal Musings*. The following year, she achieved top ten in the NAMI New Jersey poetry contest.

Griffin Unbowed, her first novel, will be available on August 6, 2019.

Made in the USA
Middletown, DE
22 October 2020

21506960R00106